A Baby in There!

Copyright © 2017 Marcelline Perry, D. Min.

All rights reserved. No part of this book may be used or reproduced by any means, graphic, electronic, or mechanical, including photocopying, recording, taping or by any information storage retrieval system without the written permission of the author except in the case of brief quotations embodied in critical articles and reviews.

WestBow Press books may be ordered through booksellers or by contacting:

WestBow Press
A Division of Thomas Nelson & Zondervan
1663 Liberty Drive
Bloomington, IN 47403
www.westbowpress.com
1 (866) 928-1240

Because of the dynamic nature of the Internet, any web addresses or links contained in this book may have changed since publication and may no longer be valid. The views expressed in this work are solely those of the author and do not necessarily reflect the views of the publisher, and the publisher hereby disclaims any responsibility for them.

Any people depicted in stock imagery provided by Thinkstock are models, and such images are being used for illustrative purposes only.
Certain stock imagery © Thinkstock.

ISBN: 978-1-9736-0565-2 (sc)
ISBN: 978-1-9736-1190-5 (hc)
ISBN: 978-1-9736-0566-9 (e)

Library of Congress Control Number: 2017915213

Print information available on the last page.

WestBow Press rev. date: 12/6/2017

A Baby in There!

Marcelline Perry, D. Min.

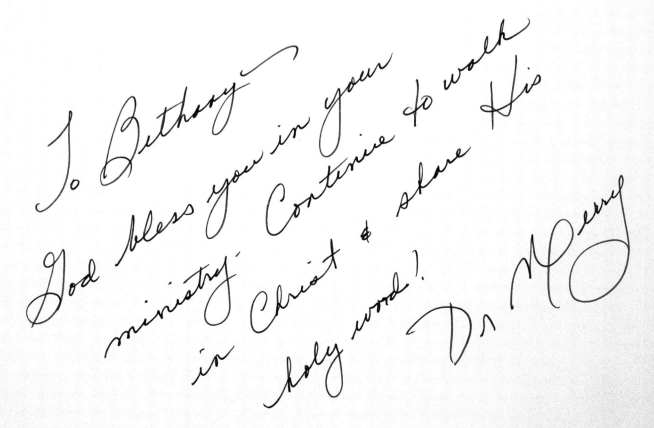

I discovered early on that all babies are special.
Each one blessed with amazing potential.
Created with differing gifts from above,
To remind the world of God's generous love.

Still, I really had no way of knowing
That inside Mommy's tummy a baby was growing.
Yet, with each passing day, I became more aware
That God had made a baby in there.

In Baby's **first month** of life I was told,
When Baby was about three weeks old,
A strong, loving heart was already beating.
Thump - THUMP. Thump - THUMP. Like a musical greeting.

By the **second month** of life my baby could stretch,
With legs that could kick and arms that could fetch.
I found out my baby felt pain and knew fear.
So, we sang soothing songs that Baby could hear.

At **two and a half months**, I learned a great fact.
Babies like mine were completely intact,
With a brain and a stomach and eyes that looked blue,
And on each tiny finger were fingerprints, too.

With each passing day, I became more aware
That God had made a baby in there.

Around the **third month** of life Mom's tummy was showing
A cute little bump where Baby was growing.
Mommy held me up close and said, "Pretty soon,
Your best friend is coming. We need to make room."

So, we painted the nursery with bears and bows.
Emptied boxes labeled "Baby" filled with blankets and clothes.
Covered a dresser with diapers, booties, bottles, and more.
Then we hung up this sign on my baby's door.
(Shhh! Baby Sleeping.)

During the **fourth month** of life at the doctor with Mom
We watched Baby moving and sucking its thumb.
This special photo of Baby was given to me,
Which I keep in a box of my memories.

By the **fifth month** I noticed Baby had grown quite a bit.
Mommy laughed because she said her pants did not fit.
It seemed only yesterday my baby was ever so small.
Now Baby had become as big as a ball.

At **six months**, I knew Baby loved me so much.
Baby jumped and moved in response to my touch.
Whenever I talked my baby tumbled around.
If I left the room, Baby settled back down.

With each passing day, I became more aware
That God had made a baby in there.

In the **seventh month** of life my baby did something so funny.
I felt Baby hiccup in Mommy's round tummy.
I was rather surprised at the feeling it made.
Like a tiny drum tapping within a parade.

Near the **eighth month** I drew a flying angel bear,
To watch over Baby with heavenly care.
A guardian angel so my baby is never alone,
Especially when I am away from our home.

As the rest of the month seemed to pass along fine,
I crossed off my calendar one day at a time.
But after **nine months** of waiting, I just had to shout:
"When will my baby decide to come out?"

The day finally came, can you guess who is here?
My sweet, gentle baby, so precious and dear.
Of God's many miracles created on earth,
The best one of all was my baby's birth.

With each passing day, I became more aware
That God had made **my** baby in there.

And, to honor each baby in the world everywhere,
I'm sending a hug, my love, and this prayer:
That God will keep you safe from harm's way,
And bless you forever with a happy birthday!

Author Biography

Marcelline Perry, Doctor of Ministry, writes inspirational and educational material for children and adults. She has served in various church ministries spanning many years and currently teaches faith communities how to strengthen their mission as disciples through an evangelization technique known as *Sacramental Dialogue*. Dr. Perry and her husband reside in Michigan where they raised two children and are now thoroughly enjoying their role as grandparents.